`Testimonies of a single Mother

"Nobody But God"

Laquitta Jenkins-Butler

Testimonies of a single Mother

Copyright © 2016 Laquitta Jenkins-Butler

All rights reserved

First Edition

Publication of: Irish Writing and Publishing (IWP)

Cover Design: Charles L. Hampton III

Proofing Provided by: Mrs. Stephanie McCray-Jenkins

No part of this book may be reproduced, stored in a retrieval system or transmitted in any form or by any means without the prior written permission of the author, except by a reviewer who may quote brief passages in a review to be printed in a newspaper, magazine, or journal.

ISBN: 0692659226
ISBN-13: 978-0692659229

DEDICATION

To my daughters, LaTia Hampton, Ashley Jenkins, and my four sons Perry Jenkins, James B. Jenkins II, Jonavon aka "Bubba" Farris and Robert A. L. Farris. I love each of you dearly. Without you I would not have found inspiration to trust God, even to this day, as I continue trusting in Him. Each of you bring a different joy into my life which is why I continue to fight to live. Through all our ups and downs (and there have been many) but with God on our side our family-unit continues to stand strong. I thank God for the young women and men that you all have become. You make me proud to say that I'm your mother. I couldn't have asked God for any better children then the ones He has given me. I appreciate everything that each one of you do for me and it does not go unnoticed. No matter what you do in life always remember that as long as you put God first, everything else will fall in place. You are the epitome of; "Honor thy mother and father."

Also to my husband Maurice Butler, I thank God for blessing me with you. I want you to know that I love you and you mean the world to me. Thank you for being a shoulder to lean on and strong support system in my life.

Charles Hampton III even though I give you a hard time, I want you to know I love you. I thank you for being a great son-in- law, a great husband to my daughter, and a great father to my grandsons, and I promise to stop talking about those "Jolly Ranchers" (inside joke).

To my grandsons Marquis L. Hampton, Malikai L. Hampton, Mylan L. Hampton, Mathias L. Hampton aka "Chip," James B. Jenkins III, and my only granddaughter Jayonna Marie Jones aka "My Princess." Nana loves you all and you are the greatest grandchildren ever.

CONTENTS

1	Fighting Against The System	Pg # 6
2	Bad Mouth Child	Pg # 11
3	Small Steps	Pg # 14
4	Truly Amazing	Pg # 17
5	She Slept Through It All	Pg # 21
6	Spared Life	Pg # 24
7	Bad Choice	Pg # 27
8	The Coach	Pg # 30
9	The Sick Room	Pg # 33
10	Who Was She	Pg # 36

ACKNOWLEDGMENTS

I first want to acknowledge God who has done so many great things for me. I promised God that if he gave me the platform I would tell the world all that he has done for me.

My only sibling Parish L. Jenkins my brother who means the world to me. I love you and I appreciate everything that you have done for me. I see why God only gave me one brother because the Lord knows I couldn't handle two of you. (lol) Seriously though you are the best brother a girl could ever ask for. Thank you for being the small square in the corner of the ceiling (inside joke).

My aunt Sarah R. Evans I want to thank you for your anointed prayers and the anointed telephone calls that help me make it through many many days. I truly love love love you!

My mother Mary W. Jenkins "Babysister" who stuck by me through thick and thin, I know today you're looking down on me with a big smile being happy for the woman that I have become.

My grandfather the late Rev. J.B. Jenkins whose prayers kept me through my deliverance and are still keeping me today.

My grandmother Mother Lucille Jenkins who has transcended from this life; I really don't have the words to express all I feel for you, but what I will say is I'm thankful for how you cared for me when I didn't care for myself. I want to thank God for your love, and longsuffering because you suffered long with me and showed love like none other. I never forgot the words you said to me when you told me that I needed to write a book. At that time I didn't even think I had a book in me; but over twenty years later the book is here.

My aunt Ida L. Miller before she left this life you gave me encouraging words that I will never forget. I will always hold them dear in my heart.

To my friends who God blessed to become my Pastor and first lady: Pastor William and Stephanie Meredith. Even though we praise God at different locations the love that I have for you still remains the same and I thank you for all that I learned under your tutelage. Pastor Meredith I'll never forget the phrase "You are destined for greatness" that you often spoke to our congregation. The words has had a major impact in my life, and I use it often when ministering to other people.

To my cousins Joseph and Paulette Williams, I want you to know I love you and appreciate you being there for me and my children when we needed you the most.

Irish Armstrong-Jordan last but not least who ever would have thought when we were back in Liberty Steel C.O.G.I.C. praising God together that God would have used you to help me bring my words to life. When my grandmother told me to write a book I know she didn't have a clue that it would be you helping me do it. I know she's rejoicing in heaven for the connection that we have made. Eyes haven't seen, ears haven't heard, neither has it entered into the heart of man, the things God has in store for us. Our connection is not just about a book but it is a move of God. Remember that your labor is not in vain.

May God get all the glory from this book!

KJV PSALM 34 1-3

"I will bless the Lord at all times,: His praise shall continually be in my mouth
My soul shall make her boast in the Lord: the humble shall hear thereof and be glad
Oh magnify the Lord with me and let us exalt His name together."

Chapter 1

Fighting Against the System

I was a single mother with two daughters. It all started with my youngest daughter's father wanting custody of her, and I refused to give it to him.

He called children services and told them I had no food in my house to feed my children. When children services came they found the accusation to be untrue because I had food. They didn't take my children, but now I had an open case with the system. They informed me that my youngest daughter's father had called them. I felt this situation was already working in my favor because they normally don't tell who called them.

However, at this point they're making regular home visits by sending out what they call a "homemaker." She would come in and check to make sure everything was in order at my house.

A couple years later I gave birth to my oldest son, but this case is still open with the children services and they're making periodic visits.

One day as I was in the bathroom smoking crack the homemaker knocked on the door. My mom told her to come in. I told my mom I was taking a bath, and I ran the water so they would think I was telling the truth.

Once I came out the bathroom, I was so high that the homemaker didn't seem to notice, so we talked through the visit as normal. After she left I went back in the bathroom and finished smoking.

Over the next few years I was required to go take urine test, and parenting classes, and each time I would pass. A few times they wanted to close my case but they would receive a telephone call stating I was doing drugs so they refused to close it.

Now three children later I was evicted from my home due to my drug addiction. As a result of having no where else to go I had to move in my mother's efficiency apartment. After being there for a couple months, management of the high-rise apartments where my mother was living were informed that me and my children were living with her.

The children services were called and came knocking on the door. They said that I had to place my children within twenty-four hours or they were going to take them.

I found placement for my children and the children services monitored the case. Keep in mind I never had to place my oldest daughter because she was fourteen and was allowed to stay with my mother. (I never understood that, but I thank God!)

About a month later I had a court date for the temporary custody hearing. At that time I told the magistrate that my youngest daughter needed to be with me because a girl needs to be with her mother. They informed me that she had been placed in two different homes and no one could do anything with her so they had already planned to give her back to me. I was happy about that however, this is another thing about the system I never understood; I still didn't have a place to live, which was the main reason for them taking my children in the first place.

The great part of this bad situation was that while my children were placed I still had a connection with them even down to our church that they were still able to attend.

During this time of being without my children I went into a three month program at a rehabilitation facility so I could get off drugs.

About two years later my court date came. I had now found a stable place for me and my children to live. The court ruled and they granted me all my children back except my youngest son.

According to the court system, the reason they wouldn't allow me to get my youngest son back was because they said, I wasn't capable to raise six children. I thought to myself, "Wow I can raise five children but not six."

Fighting the court system trying to get my youngest son back was like pulling teeth. My child's court appointed lawyer even recommended that my child be placed back with me. However, the judge stilled ruled in favor of the lady that my youngest son was placed with.

I later found out that she had connections with the court system. She worked for the judge and the judge's husband was her attorney. I brought this up as a conflict of interest. At that point they changed judges on the case, but the damage was already done. I didn't stand a chance against them.

I always felt that it was never about this caucasian lady really wanting my son so she could love and raise him as her own; but it was about the monies that she would receive.

My youngest son's father was paying six hundred dollars a month child support. After his father's death he received twelve hundred dollars a month until he turned eighteen years of age. At the time he was placed with her he was three months old.

Now I have five of my children back with me for about a year. Not long after that year I relapsed and I knew I had to do something to help myself.

I kept my house but shut it down and went to live at a rehab center in our city that accepted families. Me and my five children stayed there for about ninety days.

During that ninety days I can clearly remember one day sitting thinking, "If I continue on this path I am going to lose my children and never get them back again." I asked myself a question "Do I love crack cocaine more than my kids?" I knew the answer was that I loved my kids more than anything.

At that moment I went in the bedroom of the rehab and prayed and ask God to take away the desire and taste of crack cocaine from me. I didn't want to live this way and I didn't want to be without my children.

The fear of losing my children is what kept me until God delivered me

After those ninety days me and my children went back to our house which was the same house that I had relapsed in. God showed me that no matter what house I was in, if I truly wanted to be kept He could and would keep me.

Since that day I have been totally delivered from crack cocaine which has been over seventeen years. All glory goes to our God in Jesus name!

All five of my children that I raised have each graduated high school and attended college. My second youngest will graduate college in December 2016.

He has traveled across the country extensively, through academic success and favor from God, with all expenses being paid.

Nobody but God!

Golden Nugget

Fighting The System

I'm a living witness, no matter what you go through or how hard the struggle may be, as long as you put your trust in God, He will bring you out.

Even though it looks bad, and you can't see your way out; just keep your faith in God because God is faithful to us. It takes faith to step out on nothing and believe that something is there.

You may have family members on drugs and it may seem like they are never going to get it right, but please continue to love them. The Bible says with loving kindness have I drawn thee. So giving up is never an option, but do your best to love them back to life.

KJV Ephesians 6:12 "For we wrestle not against flesh and blood, but against principalities, against powers, against the rulers of the darkness of this world, against spiritual wickedness in high places."

Chapter 2

Bad Mouth Child

Before my mom passed she had many doctor appointments. Me and my children would always take her.

This particular doctor was not only my mother's doctor but he was also me and my children's doctor. As a result of my mother's handicap this doctor would sometimes make house visits.

One day me and my children were in his office waiting for him to examine her. The doctor walked through the door and spoke to all of us, like he normally does. He held out his hand trying to shake my two-year-old hand. My two-year-old began to say cussing words to him. The doctor laughed it off and continued to examine my mom.

A few months after that office visit the doctor came to my mom's house to examine her. He had a brand new bike with him. It was for my son that said the cuss words to him, and it was the day of his third birthday. I was shocked and very surprised.

From that day forward he would continually do things for him and then as the years went on he began doing for all my children.

Every Christmas he would write me a check for a thousand dollars to get all my children's Christmas gifts. When school started he would give me a thousand dollars to get school clothes. Easter he would give me five hundred dollars to shop for my children.

I put my three boys in baseball, football, and basketball, and not one year did I ever have to buy any equipment, because the nice doctor gave me the money to buy it. He even paid all their sports fees each year. When Perry went to college he bought Perry's school books. This doctor was a blessing to me in helping me over the years with my children.

Even though on that particular day my son said cussing words to our doctor; instead of the doctor getting offended he choose to bless!

I believe it's important to treat people nice. I always treated our doctor nice from the day I met him. I believe if I had been rude to our doctor for any reason, I would have never got the blessing that God intended for me to have.

I thank God for allowing our doctor to help my children. Thank you Jesus!

Nobody but God!

Golden Nugget

Bad Mouth Child

Sometimes we may feel that if the daddy is not helping us with our children and we're doing it all alone that we can't make it. I have found that God always has a ram in the bush.

God will put in your life what is needed to fill in the gap of the father's financial responsibilities without you having to reduce yourself to use your body.

In the word of God, David said, "I never seen the righteous forsaken or its seed begging bread."

I pray that we come to the knowledge that we are the seed of the righteous.

KJV Philippians 4:19 "But my God shall supply all your needs according to his riches in glory by Christ Jesus."

Chapter 3

Small Steps

In 1994 while visiting my mom in the hospital, the nurse was teaching my mom how to check her sugar. I was sitting there paying attention to what she was telling my mom, while drinking a gallon of orange juice that I was carrying around because I was so thirsty. While listening l began playing around with the glucose machine and checked my sugar. The reading said the word "High."

The nurse looked at me and said, "That means your sugar is over five-hundred and that's high, you should go to the ER."

Once I got downstairs to the ER they checked my blood and my sugar level was over eight hundred! They told me that it's a miracle that I'm not in a comma with a level that high, they immediately admitted me.

I stayed in the hospital for about a week while they got my sugar regulated and put me on insulin. From that day forward I have had challenges in my body from the diabetes.

In 2007 I was walking down the stairs and I felt something pop in my right ankle. I went to the hospital but they told me that no bones were broken in my ankle. Over the next few years I continued to have pain in the same ankle.

Two years later the same foot had swollen up so bad that I went to see a podiatrist. She told me that my ankle was broke and it was an old brake; she also said all the bones in my ankle were crushed. The podiatrist told me because of the diabetes, I have what is called 'Charcot Joint' which is why the bones in my ankle crushed.

My leg bone has shifted which gives my leg no support and makes it sit on the side of my foot because there's no ankle.

Even though I'm in a wheel chair I can get up and take small steps. To this day the doctors are amazed that I am able to get up from time to time, and take these steps, because most people with this type of condition are not able to walk at all.

Nobody but God!

Golden Nugget

Small Steps

In life I have come to learn that we can bring things such as sickness, and disease on ourselves by the way we eat, live and treat our bodies whether it's with drugs, alcohol etc. Even if a disease is hereditary we can make it worse by abusing our bodies.

We must be mindful of how we live our lives with regards to our appetite and what we put inside our bodies.

God is a healer in spite of what ailment or condition that we may face. The scripture says: **KJV Psalms 34:19** "Many are the afflictions of the righteous but the Lord delivereth him out of them all."

It's good to know He'll be there whenever we fall but it's also good to know that we don't have to fall at all.

Chapter 4

Truly Amazing

I went to the hospital for a stomach ache and while waiting in one of the ER examination rooms I had to use the restroom. They asked if I needed a wheelchair, and I told them no. My husband proceeded to walk me to the restroom.

While walking down the hall I felt something pop in my left leg and I couldn't move at all, then I heard the nurse shout, "Oh my God your bleeding." I saw blood all over the floor, and they said it was coming from the wound on the back of my ankle. They got towels trying to stop the bleeding, but it was so much blood that it was quickly saturating the towels.

They pulled the hospital bed up behind me and placed me upon it and rolled me back into the room. Once they finally got the blood stopped and addressed my stomach pain they discharged me, and told me to follow up with my wound doctor. Leaving the hospital I still didn't have a clue why the wound on my ankle had started bleeding.

When I went to the wound doctor on that following Monday he sent me for a direct admit to the hospital that was right across the street from his office. He had orders put in for the podiatry team to examine me.

After assessment with the podiatry team I found out the bleeding from the wound on my ankle was caused by a ruptured 'Achilles Tendon'.

Because the wound was infected they took me to surgery to clean the wound out and attached a wound-vac.

After surgery I was discharged to a nursing home to recover.
While in the nursing home I started getting sick and they found out through my blood work that my blood count was dropping. When the results came back and showed that my blood count was a five which is very low being that a normal blood count for a woman is between twelve and fifteen, they transported me back over to the hospital.

When I got to the hospital they told me to prepare to lose my leg because the infection had spread up to my leg. My leg was so infected they had to remove my Achilles Tendon due to the infection hidden behind it.

During the procedure they got enough infection out of my leg to fill up a small basketball. The next day they took me back to surgery and this time they took enough infection out to fill up an eight-ounce glass.

They told me that in the next couple days they would have to take me back to surgery to put a cement block in my leg that would release antibiotics periodically.

Before the surgery they checked my laboratory work again and thanks be to God the IV antibiotic they already had me on was clearing up the infection and my white blood count was going back to normal.

A couple days later a nurse came in my room to change my dressing on my leg. When she took the old dressing off she said, "With you being a diabetic I'm amazed how your leg is already beginning to heal so quickly."

The midnight nurse came in my room that evening and looked at my chart on the mobile computer. He said, "You're amazing, we have never seen anybody start healing this fast." I looked at him and said, "God is amazing!"

Even though my wound was healing it was wide open and in such bad condition that a regular surgeon was not able to perform the surgery to close it, but a plastic surgeon was needed.

Once the plastic surgeon came in to see me he said he may do a skin graft to close it up. I was given an appointment to go to his office in a couple weeks.

Within the next day or so I was transported back to the nursing home. On my appointment date for the plastic surgeon I was taken by ambulance to his office.

He walked in and looked at my leg and said, "Your leg is already starting to close up, there's no sense in causing you another wound so come back in four weeks."

I went back in four weeks and he said, "Your leg is still continuing to close up so we are going to see if it will continue to do it on it's own."

From that day forward my leg continued to close on its own.

Nobody But God!

Golden Nugget

Truly Amazing

We go to the doctors when we have sickness or affliction, and rightly so, we should. They have the knowledge and education to fix whatever our problem may be.

When the doctors have gone as far as their knowledge and education can take them, that's when God steps in. Man's extremity is God's opportunity.

We are grateful for physicians and the knowledge and the ability that God allows them to acquire. However we know there is no question that God is the greatest physician there is and ever will be. Hallelujah!

When the doctors told me to prepare to lose my leg the Greatest Physician said, "Not so, the wound will close on its own!"

Be encouraged to know that the doctors have come a long way with the knowledge God allows them to acquire, but God has the final word.

KJV James 5:14 "Is any sick among you? Let him call for the elders of the church."

Chapter 5

She Slept Through It All

Me, James and my granddaughter Jayonna planned to spend New Year's in Charlotte, NC with my daughters Ashley, and LaTia.

We all got in the car about 6:00 o'clock a.m. with my son Perry driving to meet my daughters in West Virginia where we would ride the rest of the way into Charlotte with them. It was freezing cold and the sun had not come up yet.

James asked Perry if he was alright to keep driving and Perry said that he was straight. We were driving along listening to the music and before I knew it Perry had ran off the highway onto the rocky, grass divider.

I began to feel the car being unleveled, and very bumpy; I started screaming, and hollering.

As Perry is trying to get back on the highway, there's a semi-truck coming that he doesn't see. Perry hit the semi-truck, with the front end passenger side of the car, which was the side I was sitting on. The car got hooked onto the semi-truck, the front and back air bags opened up, and all the back windows busted out, as the semi knocked us back off the highway.

Once the car stopped moving Perry asked us if everyone was ok and we all said yes. Perry double checked to make sure we were all ok. He then got out to see what damage was done to the car.

The truck driver was about three hundred feet down the highway, He got out of his truck and walked down to checked on us.

After a while the highway patrol showed up and came to the car and saw the windows were busted out the car. He asked me if I would like to get into his patrol car out of the cold. I told the patrol officer "No thank you, I don't get into police cars."

He asked Perry about his license and insurance. Perry's license was suspended but he did show a copy of his insurance information on his telephone, but it was lapsed. The highway patrol officer told Perry to get his license restored asap. He did charge Perry with reckless driving, but didn't take Perry to jail. The officer never even noticed that we had a baby in the car, which was a blessing because she was not in a car seat.

The car was totaled and the baby slept through the entire accident, she literally never woke up.

My husband and my friend Noelle came to the accident site and picked us up. By New Year's Eve service I was in church praising God that everyone in the accident including the semi-truck driver was alive! None of us had broken bones, not even a scar from an accident that left our car totaled.

Nobody But God!

Golden Nugget

She Slept Through It All

Even though sometimes in life you know that you're wrong in what you're doing, but thank God for His mercy.

God protects us during the seen and the unseen dangers. Though we shouldn't be alive to tell how God brought us out, but through His mercy and favor He allows us to come out on the other side giving us what we don't deserve.

There is not and never will be anyone that can give us another chance like God through his loving Son Jesus Christ!

KJV Lamentations 3:22-23 "It is of the LORD's mercies that we are not consumed, because his compassions fail not. They are new every morning: great is thy faithfulness."

Chapter 6

Spared Life

There was a lady that I have known for a long time. She was my baton teacher when I was a little girl.

During my addiction we would get high together and one day I asked her to take me to get some crack.

She and her male cousin came and picked me up and took me to buy the crack. I bought a hundred dollars' worth. I gave her some for taking me to get it.

After giving it to her she had the nerve to say, "We gettin' all that" I said "No y'all ain't." She drove down the street yet arguing with me still saying they're going to take my dope, and I'm still telling her "no y'all ain't."

I opened the car door to jump out. When I went to jump out her cousin that was sitting in the back seat reached up over the passenger side and grabbed me by the collar.

Now I'm hanging out the car and he's leaning over the seat holding my jacket collar as she is driving while dragging me. Yep, I was being dragged, but I would not let go of my dope.

After a little while he lost his grip on me, and I fell completely out the car and they drove off. I got up and walked over to a friend's house that stayed close by in that area, and I knocked on the door. When I got in the house I sat at her kitchen table and smoked my dope.

After a few minutes, my friend said "Quitta your leg is bleeding!" We lifted up my pants leg and all my skin was off my leg down to the white meat. It looked really bloody and nasty, but I kept sitting right in her kitchen smoking and didn't go to the hospital.

I could have easily been dead laying out on the street that night. Many times I would reflect back on that night and wonder how I made it through being dragged by a moving car, but the answer always lies in my heart.

He kept me when I was not in my right mind and couldn't keep myself. What I thought I had to have wasn't what I needed. I already had everything I needed protecting me, but I just didn't realize it.

Nobody but God!

Golden Nugget

Spared Life

Even when we're in our mess doing what we want to do, not thinking about God; yet the true and living God is always thinking about us.

God allows things to happen so we can see that He truly never leaves us and He will not give up on us.

Jesus says: "I will never leave thee, nor forsake thee," (Hebrew 13:5).

Something may have a hold on us that's' stronger than we are, but there is nothing stronger or more powerful than our God!

A well known artist wrote a song that goes…

"I could have been dead sleeping in my grave, but God blessed me to see another day. Even when I did wrong He was still there don't you know that God still hears a sinners prayer."

Chapter 7

Bad Choice

One particular month during my addiction the first of the month fell on a Sunday so my check came on a Friday. I smoked up my check and was still wanting to get high.

At this point I went over to the spot and got some more crack on credit from a dude that was there, because he knew I got a SSI check at the beginning of each month, I was good for it.

That whole weekend I kept going back for more and more credit. In total I had smoked about seven hundred dollars up in dope.

That following Monday the guy that I had got the credit from came to my house to take me to cash my check so he could get his money. I told him the mailman had not come yet. I was trying to think of my next move because I knew I didn't have one dime of that man's money.

He came back a few hours later, because mail had been delivered at the spot which was down the street from me.

When he knocked on my door I was scared out my mind because I knew he was going to kill me. I made a bad choice and took my son with me in hopes that he would not kill me in front of my child.

We pulled into the grocery store on the other side of town where I normally cash my check. Before I put my hand on the doorknob to get out his car I told him the truth. I said, "I got my check Friday and I already spent the money, please don't kill me in front of my son."

He cuss me out and called me all kind of names, he even said I should kill you and your son. I was so scared; he had a real serious look on his face and said, "For the next six months your food stamps belong to me." In a trembling voice I quickly said, "Ok."

He drove me and my son back to my house and said he would be back on the first of the month. He did come knocking on my door on the first of the next month, and I let him in. He said, "I ain't gonna take all your food stamps because you got kids but three hundred dollars of those food stamps is mine." So I gave him the three hundred dollars for that month.

The first of the next month came and I knew he would be coming, and for the safety of me and my kids I was prepared to give him the food stamps.

You may not believe it, but I tell you no lie; to this day I never saw that man again, and that was over seventeen years ago.

Nobody but God!

Golden Nugget

Bad Choice

When a person has an addiction, the drug is so powerful that it makes you do things that you would never do in your right mind. The drugs alters your mind and your mood.

When I was smoking all that man's stuff I knew I didn't have the money to pay for it, but my mind was telling me that I needed the drugs and I needed more and more of it.

I made the terrible choice to take my son with me knowing that the man was probably going to kill me. My mind went into a salvation mode, making me think if my child was with me the man wouldn't kill me. Truth is you cannot think clearly when you're in an addiction.

Out of everything I went through in my addiction, this situation hurts me and brings me to tears even to this day. I know how much I love my children and everyone that knows me would agree with that. The addiction will have you totally out of control, to the point of being a slave to the drug

It could have only been God that touched that man and kept him from hurting me, because in most cases me and my child would have been killed

More than anything I thank God for delivering me from the drugs. In His word He says "He will make a way of escape," and I'm a witness that He is a God that does not lie.

KJV 1 Corinthians 10:13 "There hath no temptation taken you but such as is common to man: but God is faithful, who will not suffer you to be tempted above that ye are able; but will with the temptation also make a way to escape, that ye may be able to bear it."

Chapter 8

The Coach

During the time of being totally delivered from crack cocaine I was volunteering at a Sober house in my home town. The father of my two youngest children was in the hospital about twenty miles from my home-town due to a stroke.

At this time my three oldest sons were dedicated to playing baseball and I would always do my best to have them at every practice and game on time.

One day my oldest son had a baseball game scheduled. Me and my kids pulled out the parking lot of my apartment complex and I drove about a block down the road and my car just stopped moving. I found out it was my tire rod that had broken.

I left my car and walked back to my apartment and had my neighbor take us to the game. When we arrived we were late. I told the coach what happened and asked him if my son could still play, the coach said yes.

My neighbor stayed with us while they played the game, after the game was over the coach came up to me. He asked me, "What do you have to do throughout the day." I told him that I take my kids to school, I go to the sober house that my cousin has where I volunteer and then I leave there and go to the hospital and visit my kids father, after that I come home and take my kids to practice.

He said to me, "I have a van that I can probably let you use, I can bring it to you tomorrow if you can tell me where you're going to be."

I told him that he can bring it to the sober house because that's where I would be at. He told me that he and his wife would drop it off to me tomorrow and I gratefully said ok.

It was shocking to me that this man would offer to let me use one of his vehicles; when he had just met me a month ago when I signed my boys up for baseball and he became my oldest son's coach.

The next day he came to the sober house and one of the girls came and got me. I went outside and there stood his wife along side him. Next to them was parked a Mini-Astro Van that was really nice and very clean.

He looked at me and asked, "Do you want this thing." I didn't know whether to scream or holler so I quickly said, "Yea!" He said, "It's yours." I was so shocked, I didn't know whether to hug the man or what. In excitement I said, "Thank you, thank you."

I got in the minivan and not only was it nice and clean, but all the cup holders in the van was filled up with nothing but quarters. I mean every cup holder was full.

He told me that he would be back on that following Monday to get the title signed over into my name.

When I got back in the Sober House I let loose and begin screaming and praising God.

Nobody but God!

Golden Nugget

The Coach

When you think it's all over God will step in and show you that He is God!

You may be expecting your blessing to come one way but God has something totally different just for you. God will use who you least expect to be your blessing. I would have never thought the caucasian gentlemen would be willing to let me use, let alone give me a vehicle.

It's so important to listen and follow the leading of God, because if I had not been led to take my sons so far away from where I lived to sign up for baseball I would have never got that blessing.

Never feel like you are in this by yourself because God is with you and will hold your hand and walk you through it. When you feel weak He will pick you up and carry you.

I'm not saying something that I heard but I'm telling you what I know. Real Talk.

I'm a living witness that God will give us cars that we didn't buy.

Walking in the favor of God or as I say; walking in the "fog" has many rewards and blessings that we don't ever see coming.

KJV Matthew 28:20 "Lo, I am with you always even until the end of the world. Amen"

Chapter 9

The Sick Room

A few years ago in the month of October I had two surgeries on my right foot because the doctors were trying to stop the infection. After each one of these surgeries when they woke me up out of recovery I was told that I had coded and was quickly brought back to life.

Still in the month of October because the first two surgeries were unsuccessful the doctor decided to take me back to surgery, to completely close the wound.

Because I had already coded I was afraid to have the third surgery. The fear had gripped me, but I knew I needed the surgery.

They took me from my hospital bed and rolled me down to surgery. On the way I was praying and asking God to bring me through because I was terrified to go through those doors.

I woke up in Recovery, and I remember the nurse giving me some crackers and juice.

After a while, they rolled me back down to the room, and there waiting for me was my, daughter Latia, my Son Bubba, my husband, Maurice and grandson, Marquis.

The dietary aide brought a tray of food to my room. I began to eat a cookie off the tray while talking to my husband and my kids.

The next thing I remember I seen doctors and nurses standing around my bed, one of the nurses said, "Oh you gave us a really bad scare Mrs. Butler."

I was confused because I had no idea what they were talking about, the last thing I remember is that, I was eating a cookie and talking.

When my son saw me looking confused he looked at me and said "Mommy while you was eating you passed out, and at first we thought you had fell asleep, but then we realized you were not conscious."

I looked at him like, are you serious?

He continued to say, "Maurice ran and got the nurse and doctor to come in the room. They were trying to revive you for a long time, then they said they would have to put you on a ventilator. Once they said the word "Ventilator" you opened your eyes and sat straight up in the bed."

Nobody but God!

Golden Nugget

The Sick Room

Just because people count you out does not mean you're out. It's never over until God says that it's over. God has a plan for each and every one of us and no matter what anyone else says about our life the final word comes from God.

Even though you may be down you are not defeated when you're looking to God.

KJV Romans 8:28 "And we know that all things work together for good to them that love God, to them who are the called according to His purpose."

Chapter 10

Who was She

Continuing to live out my deliverance from crack cocaine, I moved to Columbus and got engaged. My fiancée was living in my hometown about three hours away.

My niece Tamara who's a young adult moved in with me and my children. One weekend night my niece and my daughter Ashley who is close to my niece's age, wanted to go to the Nelly concert and I agreed to take them.

On my way taking them to the concert my car broke down at the gas station. I went in to tell the attendant that I needed to leave my car there until I could get somebody to look at it.

There was a caucasian lady standing there talking to the attendant and heard me tell the attendant about my car. She turned and asked me what's wrong with your car. I told her I didn't know but I was going to get someone to look at it.

She asked me where was I going, I told her I was on my way to take my daughter and niece to a concert. She came outside where my car was and said, "Oh you got other kids in the car with you too."

She then said, "I'll tell you what, I live across the street and I have a car that you can use to take your children where they have to go." Me and my kids walked with her across the street and got her car.

I took Ashley and Tamara to the concert and I brought her car back. She asked, "What all do you have to do tomorrow?" I told her I have to go to work the next night because I worked midnights. She said, "Well, since you have to pick the kids back up tonight, you can keep my car until tomorrow and I will have my son look at your car, because he works on cars."

She called me the next day and said her son wasn't able to fix my car, but she had it taken to a shop and it would cost five hundred dollars for the repairs.

I was shocked and didn't know how I was going to get it fixed, but before I could say anything she told me not to worry because she had it under control. She told me to keep her car so I could go to work that night, and bring it back after I get off work the next morning.

I took her car back to her after I got off work the next morning, She told me that my car would be ready in a couple days, she then asked me what was my work schedule and I told her. I also told her that I go to my hometown on the weekend because I'm planning my wedding.

She told me to go ahead and keep her car to get back and forth to work. She also told me that when I get ready to go to my hometown I was to bring her car back to her, and she would let me drive her brand new mustang to my hometown.

That following week my car was ready she brought it to me and took her car.

Two weeks later my car got repossessed. I called her and told her what happened and asked her if I could get a ride to work. She came over and brought me back the car that I was driving. She allowed me to drive it to work and take my kids where they had to go during this time. Then on the weekends she still allowed me to drive her mustang to my hometown.

When I got married she furnished all my flowers and my center pieces for my weeding. After me and my husband married he was working at a steel mill and I was working at the nursing home.

This same lady went and bought us a van so we would have transportation to get back and forth to work.

To this day I have not seen or heard from this lady again. I did go back to her house but she had moved out. From time to time I try to find her but I still have not been able to locate her. It's like she never existed but I know without a doubt it was very real.

Nobody but God!

Golden Nugget

Who Was She

It's very important to be mindful how you treat people. I could have been rude to the lady when we first met at the gas station when she asked me about my car. It was like she was getting into my business but I didn't take that approach.

I remember my grandmother told me that it's just nice to be nice, and if you be nice to somebody, then somebody will be nice to you.

We must be careful how we treat people because you never know who your angel might be. The person that you disrespect or treat bad could very well be your angel and you would miss your blessing.

The scripture below is what I have always instilled in my children. As a result of my children applying this scripture to their lives they have received many wonderful blessings.

We must not mistake people being nosey, because they may really care about what's going on with you. Even more than that they could be on an assignment to help you.

KJV Hebrews 13:2: "Be not forgetful to entertain strangers: for thereby some have entertained angels unawares."

Words to my Readers

Thank you for taking time to read my testimonies and allowing me to share a part of my life with you.

My purpose for writing this book is for God to get the glory!

In sharing my testimonies I want to let people know that God is REAL and the things that happened in my life are real. I have found that God is the same today as he was in Biblical times, and the power that he showed in those times is the same power that he show's today.

As you can see from my testimonies my second chance ran out a long time ago, but I have come to know God to be a God of another chance.

To any reader that is going through what I've been through or any similar issues; I want you to know that there is no secret what God can do. What he has done for me, He can do the same for you.
Real talk.

My goal is to encourage single mothers and to let them know; that no matter what you go through, if you keep God in the forefront of your life he will see you through.

As a single mother with six children and five fathers, raising my children seemed impossible without the father's being there, but with God all things are possible.

While fighting that drug addiction it was God that helped me raise my children to be productive young men and women.

Allow me to share the scripture with you that helped me through: **KJV Philippians 4:13** "I can do all things through Christ that strengthens me."

While walking this road things don't always look good or feel good. I encourage you to believe and have faith that God will see you through

God is there but He's not a thief or a robber. He's not going to break in; but if you open up your heart to Him and let him come in; He will straighten up the crocked place in your life.

I challenge you to give Him a try! He will never fail you, even though you may be in a place in your life where you feel that you're not worthy. God has already showed us that we are worthy because He died for us

I know that there's other women out there that have multiple children by multiple fathers like myself. You may feel like I have all these children and I can't do this on my own. Baby, I'm a living witness, if you put God in the mix you can make it!

Even though I was not professing salvation during some of these testimonies. I've always had a strong faith and belief in God and He always had His hand on my life.

KJV Ephesians 3:20 "Now unto Him that is able to do exceeding abundantly above all that we ask or think according to the power that worketh in us."

ABOUT THE AUTHOR

She is a mother of six children. After leaving high school, she went on to receive her GED and went to college. With much study and hard work she graduated with her Associate's Degree.

After being a single mother for many years and raising her children; God blessed her with a wonderful husband, Maurice Butler.

She currently attends Greater Liberty Temple Church of God in Christ in Columbus Ohio under the leadership of Bishop David L and First Lady Brenda Herron.

Each testimony shared in this book was lived out by the author between the years of 1988-2015

Laquitta is in the process of completing her next book, putting her life story into words that many will be inspired. This book is due to be released in the next few months

Her motto for life is: "Falling in love with Jesus is the best thing I ever done!"

"They overcame him by the blood of the lamb and the words of their testimony."

KJV Revelation 12:11

All Biblical verses used in this book are quoted in consistency from the King James Version Bible.

www.ingramcontent.com/pod-product-compliance
Lightning Source LLC
Chambersburg PA
CBHW060622070426
42449CB00042B/2401